LOGIC PUZZLES
for
Clever Kids!

Fun brain games for ages 4 & up

LOGIC PUZZLES

for

Clever Kids!

by Molly Lynch

R

ROCKRIDGE
PRESS

Interior and Cover Designer: Emma Hall
Art Producer: Hillary Frileck
Editor: Mary Colgan
Production Editor: Andrew Yackira

Designed and illustrated by Creative Giant Inc., Mike Thomas, Chris Dickey, Paul Tutrone.
Illustrated by Wolfe Hanson

ISBN: Print 978-1-64611-013-1

Chapter 1
Sequencing

Sequencing is the ability to understand and logically order images, actions, events, or thoughts. Through sequencing, children learn about patterns and how things are organized. In this chapter, you will guide your child through various puzzles to help them develop these important skills.

First, Second, or Third?

Write a 1, 2, or 3 under the pictures to show the correct order.

Answer on page 70

Parent Prompt

Encourage your child to expand their thinking beyond the third picture. Ask, "If there were one more picture, what might it be?"

Rhyme Time!

Read the nursery rhyme aloud. Encourage your child to add details to the picture to match the words of the rhyme.

Jack and Jill went up the hill
to fetch a pail of water.
Jack fell down and broke his crown,
And Jill came tumbling after.

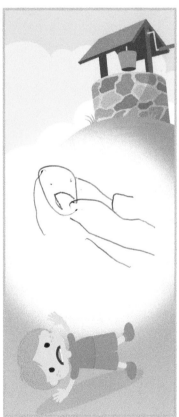

Answer on page 70

Parent Prompt

Reread the nursery rhyme. Encourage your child to listen for the rhyming words. Ask, "Can you think of another word that rhymes with that word?"

Silly Scribbles

Write the numbers 1 to 4 to show the order of the drawings.

Monster

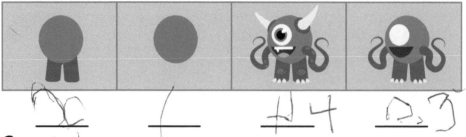

____ ____ ____ 4 ____ 3

Car

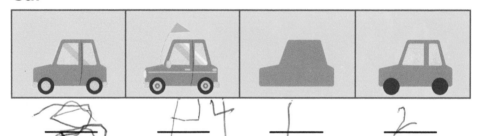

____ ____ 4 ____ ____ 2

Dinosaur

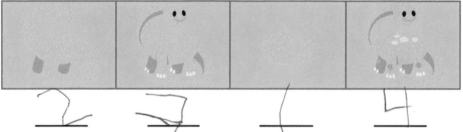

____ 2 ____ ____ ____

House

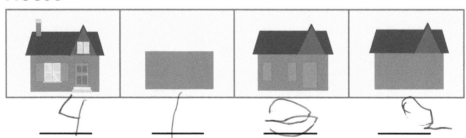

____ ____ ____ ____

Answer on page 70

Parent Prompt

Ask your child to think of another object that can be drawn in a sequence. Encourage them to describe the steps in detail as they draw it for you.

Helping at Home

Circle the picture on the right that shows what happens next.

Answer on page 70

5

Beeee Smart!

Follow the trail of numbers in order from 1 to 10 to get the bee back to her hive. There is more than one path the bee can take!

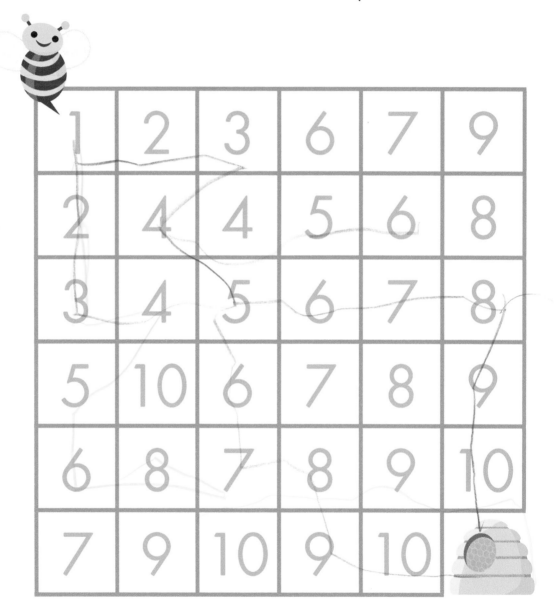

Answer on page 71

Parent Prompt

Encourage your child to look for other paths and trace each one in a different color.

Getting Ready

Look at the pictures. Write the numbers 1 through 6 to show what the girl does first, second, third, and so on.

2 4 5 3

Answer on page 71

Parent Prompt

Have your child describe their morning routine and then explain how it compares to the girl's. Ask, "How is it the same? How is it different?"

Flying Home

Follow the numbers in order from 1 to 10 to solve the maze.

Answer on page 71

Parent Prompt

Encourage your child to trace the maze again with a finger starting at 10 and counting backward. You can also ask them to count forward again using ordinal numbers (first, second, third, etc.).

All Aboard

Write the missing numbers.

| 1 | 2 | 3 | 4 | 5 | 6 |

| 10 | 9 | 8 | 7 | 6 | 5 |

| 5 | 6 | 7 | 8 | 9 | 10 |

| 2 | 4 | 6 | 8 | 10 | 12 |

Answer on page 71

Parent Prompt

To extend this activity, give your child another initial number. Each of you can take turns saying one number in the sequence. For example, "Let's count up starting at 3. What number comes next? And then?"

Chapter 2
Comparisons & Abstract Thinking

Learning to think abstractly is an important part of developing problem-solving skills. In the early years, children understand ideas and concepts on a concrete level through their own experiences. As they develop, they are able to apply their experiences in a broader, more complex way, thinking beyond the world that's in front of them. Giving your children many opportunities to compare and classify objects will strengthen their problem-solving abilities and help them analyze the world around them. In the following puzzles, your child will use real-world knowledge to find solutions.

Travel All Year

Imagine you're taking a trip each season. Cross out the item you would not need or see in that season.

Winter

Spring

Summer

Fall

Answer on page 72

Parent Prompt

Seasons can be tricky for your child to understand because they have a limited understanding of time. You may need to prompt your child with ideas or memories you've shared in a particular season. Ask, "Which season is your favorite and why? What else would you add to the suitcase? What else would you not need in the suitcase?"

A Day in the Park

Spot the three differences between the two pictures.
Circle what is different in the bottom picture.

Answer on page 72

Parent Prompt

Encourage your child to add a few pictures to each park scene, making sure they are different. Ask your child, "What are some things that you see at the park that may change?"

Pizza Party!

Cross out the toppings you would probably not find on a pizza.

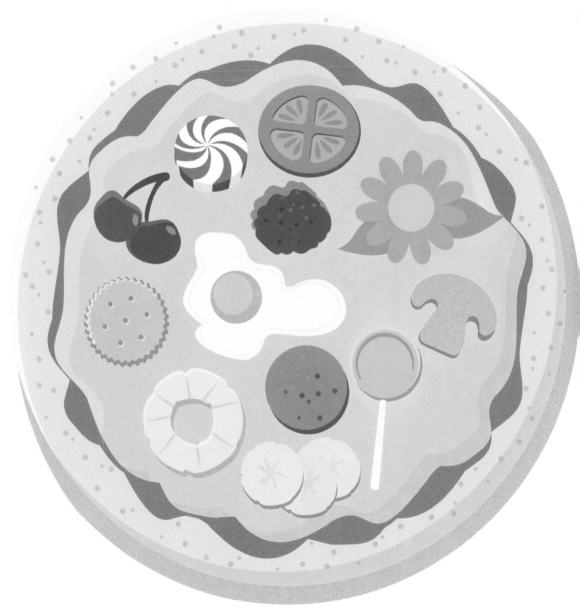

Answer on page 72

Parent Prompt

Ask your child, "Can you think of any other toppings that we can add to the pizza? What other toppings would be silly to add to the pizza?"

Shape Up

Cross out the object that does not belong in each row.

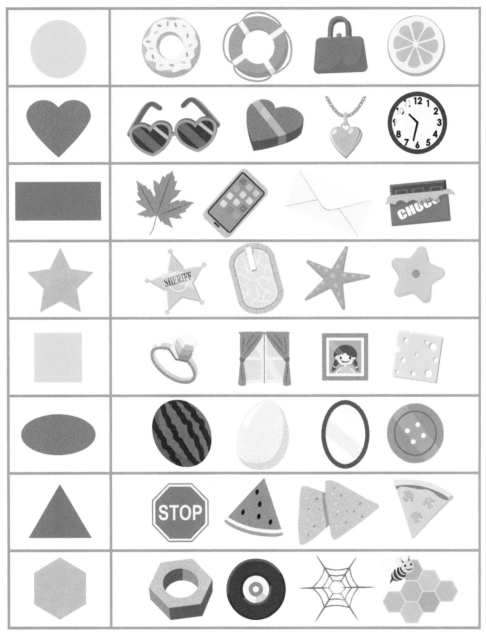

Answer on page 72

Parent Prompt

Invite your child to count the number of sides and corners on each shape as you say the name. You can also say, "Look around the room. What shapes do you see?"

A Fridge Hunt

Circle the items that **belong** in the refrigerator. Cross out the items that **do not belong** in the freezer.

Answer on page 73

Parent Prompt

Ask your child, "Why don't we keep popcorn in the refrigerator? Why don't we put crackers in the freezer?"

Tip the Scale

Circle the object that is lighter.

Circle the object that is heavier.

Draw an object to match the scale. Look at how the scale is tipped to see which side is heavier.

Answer on page 73

Parent Prompt

Name an object in your home. Ask your child, "What is something that is lighter than this?" Name another object and ask, "What is something that is heavier than this?" Encourage your child to weigh the objects in their hands as if they are a human scale!

Butterflies!

Write the number of each kind of butterfly in the circles.

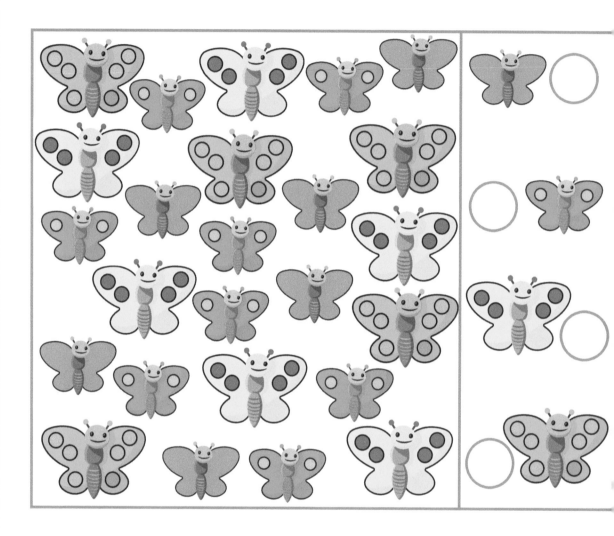

Answer on page 73

Parent Prompt

Encourage your child to cross out each butterfly as they count. This will help your child to correctly track the number using one-to-one correspondence. After filling in the totals, ask, "Which kind of butterfly has the most? Which kind of butterfly has the least?"

Snack Time!

Follow the shape path to find out what each child will eat for a snack.

Answer on page 73

Parent Prompt

Ask your child to think of other foods that are shaped like an apple or a carrot.

Chapter 3
Inferences

Inferences are what we figure out based on what we already know. Children look at clues from pictures and words to figure out what is happening, what has already happened, or what may happen. As your child develops, drawing inferences will become an important part of being a reader. In this chapter, guide your child to solve the puzzles to improve their skill in coming to conclusions and making inferences.

Rain or Shine

Draw a line to what you may need for the weather shown.

Answer on page 74

Parent Prompt

Ask your child to look out the window and explain everything they would need to wear for today's weather.

Animal Riddles

Draw a line to the animal that solves the riddle.

I slither on the ground.
I hiss and curl up in the sun.

I like to swing from trees.
You can find me in the jungle.

I'm a bird who cannot fly.
Instead, I love to swim!
I often live in cold places.

I have a large mane.
People call me the king of the jungle.

I hop around.
I live near lakes, ponds, and streams.

I travel very slowly.
I wear my home on my back.

Answer on page 74

Parent Prompt

Tell your child to imagine an animal. Say, "Give me one clue about the animal you thought of so I can guess what it is!" Take turns thinking of an animal and giving clues to each other.

Asking Questions

Underline the question that makes sense based on the picture.

"Do you want a bottle?"
"Do you want to play outside?"

"Do you want to play ball?"
"Can we get an ice cream?"

"Can we play at the park?"
"Should we return our books?"

"Do you want to go for a bike ride?"
"Do you want to eat lunch?"

"Should we visit Grandma?"
"Are you ready to swim?"

"Can you brush your teeth?"
"Ready for the story?"

Answer on page 74

Parent Prompt

Reread the sentence that did not fit the picture. Say to your child, "Tell me about a picture that would match that sentence."

What's Happening?

Look at each picture and answer the questions.

Why is the firetruck there?

Why is the woman stopping?

Why is the sprinkler on?

Why is the boy covering his ears?

Answer on page 74

Parent Prompt

Challenge your child to think of alternative scenarios. For each image, ask, "When else might (a firetruck be called; a woman get out of her car, etc.)?"

How Do They Feel?

Draw a line to match the feelings for each picture.

Omar is sad.

Annika is proud.

Tasha is surprised.

Eric is scared.

Answer on page 75

Parent Prompt

Remind your child of an event that recently happened. Ask, "How did that make you feel?" Repeat the activity to cover a range of emotions.

What Time?

Underline what time of day each picture might take place.

Morning
Afternoon
Night

Morning
Afternoon
Night

Morning
Afternoon
Night

Morning
Afternoon
Night

Morning
Afternoon
Night

Morning
Afternoon
Night

Morning
Afternoon
Night

Morning
Afternoon
Night

Morning
Afternoon
Night

Answer on page 75

Parent Prompt

Ask your child, "Can any of these events happen at another time of day besides what's shown in the picture?"

Whose Shoes?

Match the shoes to the person who wears them.

Answer on page 75

Parent Prompt

Ask your child, "What are other special shoes people wear for their jobs?" You can also ask, "Do you wear any special shoes?"

What Will It Be?

Draw a line to what the ingredients will make.

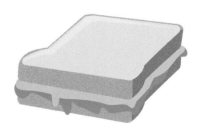

Answer on page 75

Parent Prompt

Ask your child, "What is another ingredient you can add to each picture that would make sense?"

Chapter 4
Patterns

Creating, extending, recognizing, and discussing patterns is a key foundational math skill. Working with patterns will give your child practice with visual discrimination of colors and shapes. The skill of recognizing and creating patterns helps learners make predictions based on observation, and helps them to become strong mathematicians. Guide your child through the pattern puzzles in this chapter. If your child does not see the pattern, it may be helpful to say the pattern aloud by shape or color so your child can hear it first.

Shape Patterns

Say the pattern aloud. Draw the two shapes that come next for each line.

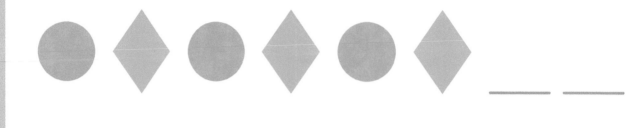

_____ _____

_____ _____

_____ _____

_____ _____

Answer on page 76

Parent Prompt

Tell your child, "Choose a couple of the shapes above and create your own pattern. Name the shapes as you make your pattern."

Building Patterns

Say the pattern aloud. Color the blocks to follow the pattern.

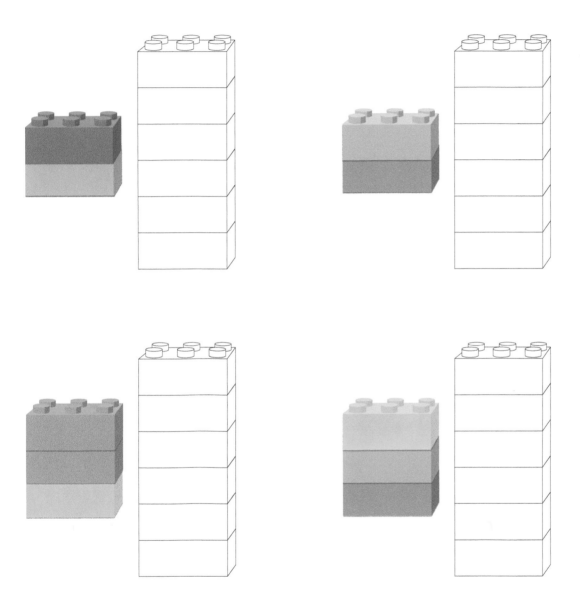

Answer on page 76

Parent Prompt

Say to your child, "Now let's come up with our own pattern. You start it, and I'll try to figure out what comes next." Take turns making color patterns. You may want to use building blocks.

Bedroom Patterns

Study the bedroom. Circle the patterns you see.

Answer on page 76

Parent Prompt

Say to your child, "Look around this room and point out any patterns you see." You may need to start by pointing out a pattern such as the tile in the kitchen or fabric on your couch.

Ice Cream

Say the pattern aloud. Color the missing scoops.

Answer on page 76

Parent Prompt

Tell your child, "My favorite ice cream flavor is _____. What's yours? Let's make a pattern with our two flavors. How many different patterns can we make with those two flavors?"

35

Picking Patterns

Draw the missing fruit based on the number pattern.

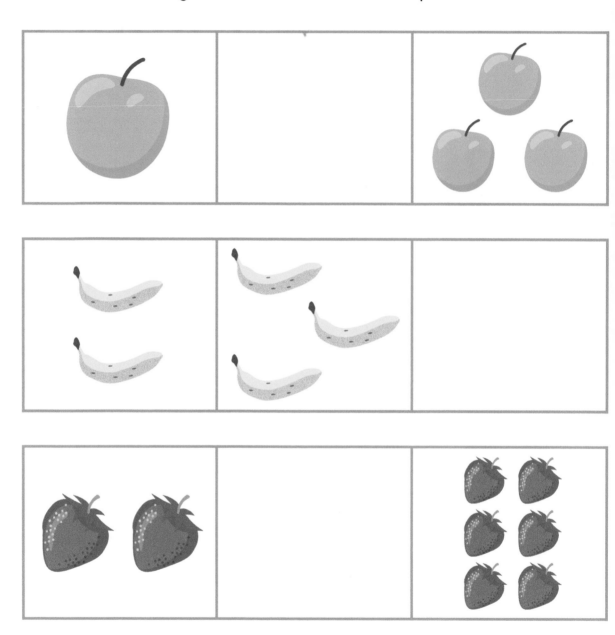

Answer on page 77

Parent Prompt

To help your child, ask questions such as, "How many are in the first box and the second box? How many in the first and last box? How many should be in between?"

Size Patterns

Fill in the next two shapes in the pattern.

Answer on page 77

Parent Prompt

It can be helpful to say aloud each pattern and include a size word, such as,
"This pattern is 'big heart, little heart, little heart.' What will come next?"

Hero Patterns

Circle the superhero that comes next in the pattern.

Answer on page 77

Pattern Blocks

Circle what the next two shapes will be.

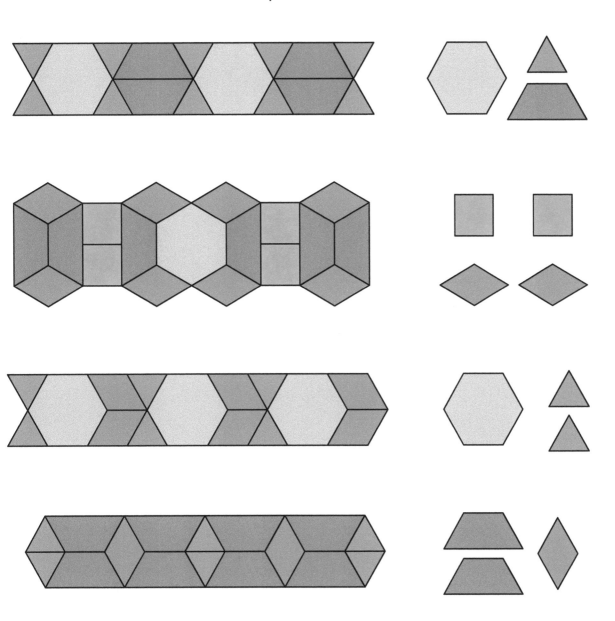

Answer on page 77

Parent Prompt

These patterns can be tricky because the shapes are angled in various ways. Help your child by naming the shapes aloud as you work through each pattern. In addition, have your child name the colors.

Chapter 5
Analogies

Analogies compare two things that have something in common but are otherwise unalike. For instance, your child can compare apples and oranges by noting that they are both fruits, but different kinds. Analogies give children the chance to practice important skills such as opposites, part versus whole, similarities and differences, and vocabulary. In this chapter, you will need to help your child see the relationship between the objects shown.

Counting Sides

Circle the correct shape that goes in the box.

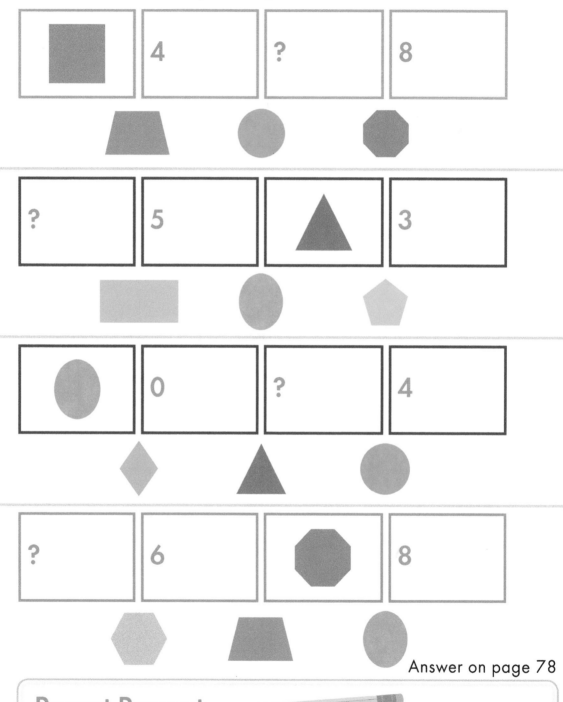

Answer on page 78

Parent Prompt

Ask your child, "Can you tell me how many sides a triangle has? Now look around the room and find something that also has three sides." Repeat this activity for various shapes.

Animal Homes

Circle the correct home for each animal.

Where does the fish live?

Where does the bee live?

Where does the polar bear live?

Answer on page 78

Parent Prompt

Name a habitat for your child. Say, "How many animals can you name that might live there?"

43

Colors and Shapes

Circle the correct answer to complete the puzzle.

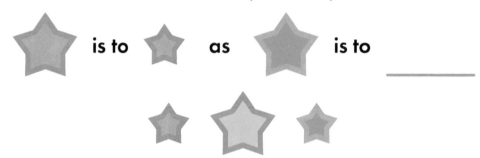

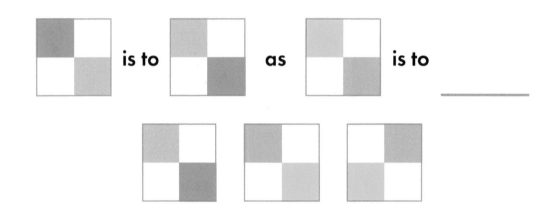

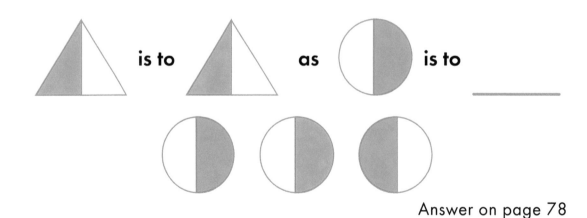

Answer on page 78

Parent Prompt

Pick two items in the room. Say to your child, "Let's compare these two things. How are they the same? How are they different?"

Nature Pairs

Draw a picture to complete the puzzle.

leaf **is to** tree **as** seed **is to** [   ]

bear **is to** cave **as** fish **is to** [   ]

cow **is to** milk **as** chicken **is to** [   ]

Answer on page 78

Parent Prompt

Pick two animals. Ask your child, "How are they the same? How are they different?"

Everyday Shapes

Circle the shape that completes the comparison.

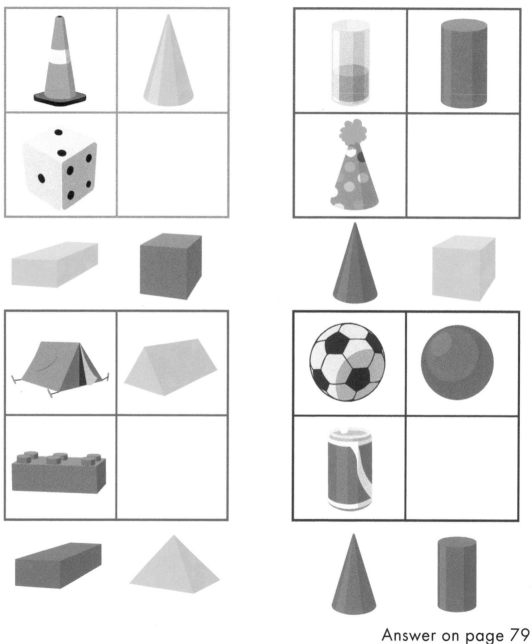

Answer on page 79

Parent Prompt

Point to a shape on the page. Ask your child, "What other objects can you think of that are shaped like this?" Repeat for all the shapes on the page.

Tool Time

Circle the correct tool for each person.

Answer on page 79

Parent Prompt

Say to your child, "Now let's think of other jobs people may have. What tools do they need to use for their job?"

Getting Dressed!

Draw a line to the picture that completes the puzzle.

 are to **as**  **are to...**

 is to **as**  **are to...**

 is to **as**  **is to...**

 are to **as**  **is to...**

 is to **as**  **is to...**

Answer on page 79

Parent Prompt

List other items you or your child may wear. Ask, "On what part of our bodies do we wear this?"

Dinnertime

Circle the correct food for the animal.

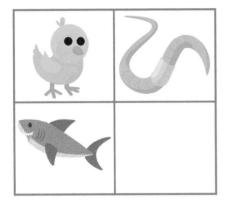

What does the shark eat?

What does the cow eat?

What does the dog eat?

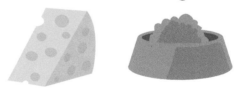

Answer on page 79

Parent Prompt

Ask your child, "What do you like to eat? What foods do you not like to eat?"

49

Chapter 6
Deduction

Deductive reasoning is a critical skill for problem solving. It requires your child to sort through a series of facts (based on pictures or text) to determine what else is true. (For instance, all dogs have fur and all golden retrievers are dogs. Therefore, all golden retrievers have fur.) Learning how to sort through information will help your child develop the ability to draw conclusions and make generalizations. In this chapter, you will guide your child through the puzzles to sort through the facts and identify the similarities and differences between the pictures.

Tutti Fruitti

Use the clues and grid to figure out each person's favorite fruit.

Dina, Luke, and Tara each like a different fruit best.

1. Luke likes fruit that does not have to be peeled.
2. Dina does not like red fruit.
3. Tara loves her fruit when it's in a pie.

Answer on page 80

Parent Prompt

As you read the clues, encourage your child to write No in a box when a clue rules it out, then write Yes when they find the right answer. To expand the conversation, ask your child what other fruits each child may like based on the clues given.

Odd Sound Out

Say the name of each item. Cross out the picture or pictures that do not begin with the letter in the circle.

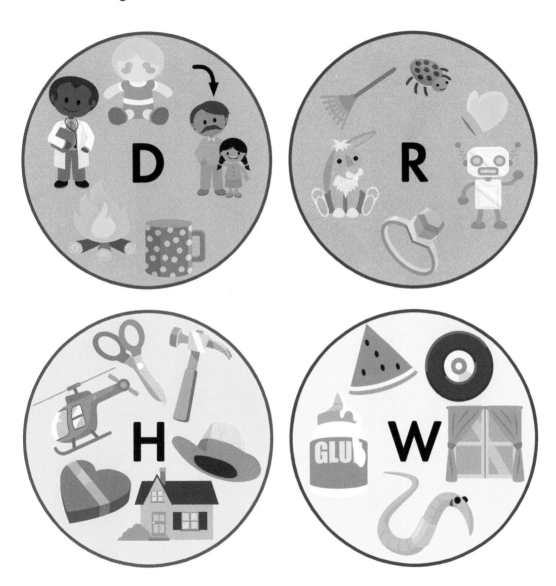

Answer on page 80

Parent Prompt

Ask your child, "What letter does your name begin with? Can you tell me three words that begin with the same sound as the first letter of your name? Now let's try to find words for the first letter of my name."

53

I Spy . . .

Circle the animal that is most like the one in the magnifying glass.

Answer on page 80

Parent Prompt

Pick two similar objects in the room (such as a couch and a chair). Ask your child, "How are these different? How are they the same?"

Animal Kingdom

Cross out the animal that is not part of the group.

Birds

Fish

Insects

Mammals

Answer on page 80

Parent Prompt

Ask your child, "When you look at each group of animals, how are they similar? How are they different? Can you think of any other animals to add to the group?"

Let's Rhyme!

In each grid, cross out the picture that does not rhyme.

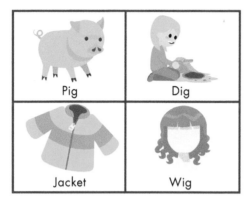

Pig | Dig | Jacket | Wig

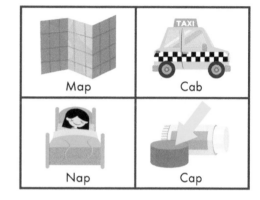

Map | Cab | Nap | Cap

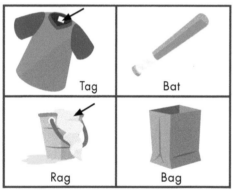

Tag | Bat | Rag | Bag

Ten | Hen | Pen | Bed

Rug | Bug | Sun | Mug

Mop | Frog | Log | Dog

Answer on page 81

Parent Prompt

Rhyming can be tricky for young learners. It may be helpful to say each word aloud for your child in an exaggerated tone. To extend the activity, choose the word from each puzzle that was not used. Ask your child, "Can you think of two words that rhyme with it?"

Dessert Time!

Use the clues to figure out each person's favorite sweet treat. After listening to the clues, draw a line to match each child to his or her favorite treat.

Mariana

Ryan

Sean

Mariana likes treats with sprinkles.

Sean's treat has a wrapper.

Ryan's treat is on a stick.

Answer on page 81

A Trip to the Zoo

Use the clues to figure out Amir's favorite animal.

It has fur.
It has four paws.
It eats fish.
It lives near cold water.

What is Amir's favorite animal?

_____

Answer on page 81

Parent Prompt

Help your child by reading the clues. Suggest that they cross out the animals based on the clues.

Categories

Add a picture to each group.

Balls

Fruits

Tools

Answer on page 81

Parent Prompt

Name another category. Ask your child, "Can you name three things that would fit in that category? What's an item that would not fit in that category?"

Chapter 7
Critical Thinking

Critical thinking is a skill that will increase throughout your child's development. A critical thinker can solve problems using known information or seek out the necessary information in order to solve the problem. Being a good critical thinker will help your child express thoughts, develop creativity, and solve problems. In this chapter, guide your child through the challenging puzzles. Your child may need your help with vocabulary or more abstract concepts, such as the cowgirl saying, "Howdy, partner," on page 64.

School of Fish

Listen to the clues to color the school of fish.

The first and last fish are orange.
The fish in the middle is black.
Both fish next to the middle fish are yellow.
The fish next to the orange fish are blue.
The third fish from the left is green.
The third fish from the right is purple.

Answer on page 82

Parent Prompt

Be sure to read one line and have the child color before you read the next line. Ask your child, "What color is the 8th fish? What number is the purple fish?" You can also ask, "What color is the fish before the green fish? Which fish comes two after the first fish?" Continue asking similar questions.

Color a Garden

Listen to the clues to color the picture.

The tallest flower is purple.
The shortest flower is orange.
The flowers on the ends are pink.
The middle flower is blue.

Answer on page 82

Answer on page 82

Parent Prompt

Ask your child to order the height of your family members from shortest to tallest. Your child can also order people from youngest to oldest.

63

Dress Up Time!

Listen to the clues. Draw a line from each person to their hat.

Leo says, "Arrrrrr!"
Matt asks, "Do you feel okay?"
Natasha says, "Howdy, partner!"
Brooke asks, "Would you like vanilla frosting?"

Natasha   Leo   Brooke   Matt

Answer on page 82

Parent Prompt

Tell your child, "Imagine you are wearing a hat for your job. What might you say? I'll try to guess what job you do." Take turns playing.

Birthday Fun

Answer the questions about birthdays.

Today is Manny's birthday and this is his cake.

How old is Manny? _____

How old was he last year? _____

How old will he be next year? _____

Now draw your dream birthday cake. Add candles for your age.

How old are you? _____

How old were you last year? _____

How old will you be next year? _____

Answer on page 82

Set the Table

The kids are setting the table for dinner! Listen to the clues.
Draw a table that is the right shape to match the clues.

Robin  Robin's table has 3 sides.

George  George's table has 4 sides. 2 are short and 2 are long.

Nadia  Nadia's table has no sides. It is round.

Max  Max's table has 4 equal sides.

Answer on page 83

Parent Prompt

Ask your child to add food to the table that matches the shape of each table. For instance, they might add a box of cereal to George's table or put an orange on Nadia's table.

Off to School!

Listen to the clues to find out how the kids get to school. Draw a line to match.

JB waits on the corner for his ride.
Susan takes the longest to get to school.
Luisa needs a helmet to get to school safely.
Caleb rides with his dad and brother.

Answer on page 83

Answer on page 83

Parent Prompt

Read each clue and stop to have your child draw the line. Then read the next clue. Tell your child how they will get to school: "When you go to school this fall, you will be like (child on page) because you will _____."

Yummy Treats

Circle the object that matches the clues given.

It grows on a tree.
It is round.
It can be used to
make juice.

It is a sweet treat.
It has frosting.
It can be cut into
pieces.

It can be a snack.
It is not crunchy.
It is found in the
refrigerator.

Answer on page 83

Parent Prompt

As you read the clues, encourage your child to cross out the objects that do not fit the clues.

Riding Bikes

Listen to the clues. Draw a line from each child to his or her bike.

Pierce's whole family can ride on one bike together.

Emma likes to pick flowers to take home.

Ethan loves the color blue.

Kathleen's doll can ride with her.

Pierce

Emma

Ethan

Kathleen

Answer on page 83

Parent Prompt

Say to your child, "Let's count the number of wheels of all the bikes and scooters we have in our home. What if we add one more bike? What if we add two more bikes?"

2 First, Second, or Third?

Correct order:

3	1	2
3	2	1
2	3	1

3 Rhyme Time!

Jack and Jill walking up the hill

Jack falling

Jill tumbling down the hill

4 Silly Scribbles

Correct order:

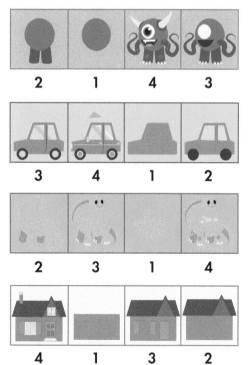

2	1	4	3
3	4	1	2
2	3	1	4
4	1	3	2

5 Helping at Home

These are the pictures that show what happens next:

6 *Beeee* Smart!

Here are two of the possible paths:

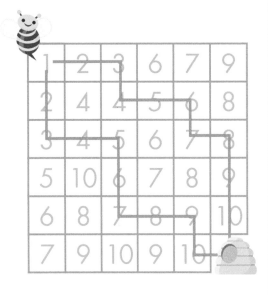

7 Getting Ready

Correct order:

8 Flying Home

9 All Aboard

12 Travel All Year

These are the items you would not see in each season:

13 A Day in the Park

Differences:

14 Pizza Party!

These are the items you would probably not find on a pizza:

15 Shape Up

These are the objects that do not belong in each row:

Row 1:

Row 2:

Row 3:

Row 4:

Row 5:

Row 6:

Row 7:

Row 8:

16 A Fridge Hunt

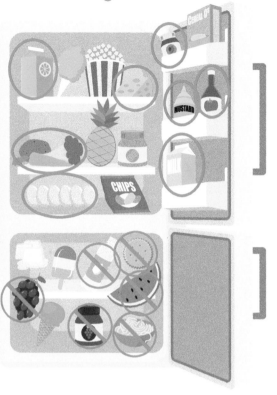

17 Tip the Scale

18 Butterflies!

 6

8

 6

5

19 Snack Time!

22 Rain or Shine

23 Animal Riddles

Clue 1:

Clue 2:

Clue 3:

Clue 4:

Clue 5:

Clue 6:

24 Asking Questions

Picture 1: "Do you want a bottle?"

Picture 2: "Can we get an ice cream?"

Picture 3: "Should we return our books?"

Picture 4: "Do you want to go for a bike ride?"

Picture 5: "Are you ready to swim?"

Picture 6: "Ready for the story?"

25 What's Happening?

Picture 1: The house is on fire.

Picture 2: She wants to buy lemonade.

Picture 3: The boy and the dog want to play in the water.

Picture 4: The music is too loud.

26 How Do They Feel?

 Eric is scared.

 Tasha is surprised.

 Omar is sad.

 Annika is proud.

27 What Time?

 Night

 Morning

 Afternoon

 Afternoon

 Morning

 Night

 Morning

 Afternoon

 Night

28 Whose Shoes?

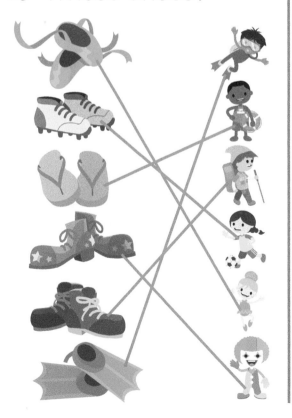

29 What Will It Be?

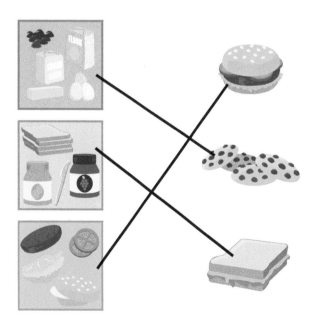

32 Shape Patterns

33 Building Patterns

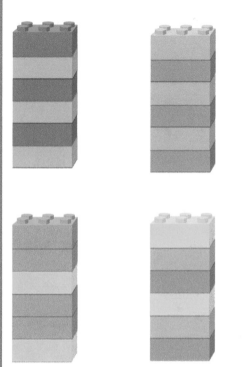

34 Bedroom Patterns

Here are some of the patterns in the picture. You may have found others.

There is a polka dot pattern on the bedspread.

There is a striped pattern on the curtains.

There is a star pattern on the wallpaper.

35 Ice Cream

36 Picking Patterns

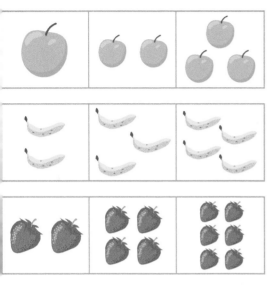

37 Size Patterns

38 Hero Patterns

Row 1:

Row 2:

Row 3:

39 Pattern Blocks

Row 1: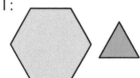

Row 2:

Row 3:

Row 4:

42 Counting Sides

Row 1:

Row 2:

Row 3:

Row 4:

43 Animal Homes

The fish lives here:

The bee lives here:

The polar bear lives here:

44 Colors and Shapes

Row 1:

Row 2:

Row 3:

45 Nature Pairs

Row 1:
a flower with pink petals

Row 2:
a fishbowl, pond, lake, or ocean

Row 3:
an egg

46 Everyday Shapes

Puzzle 1:

Puzzle 2:

Puzzle 3:

Puzzle 4:

47 Tool Time

48 Getting Dressed!

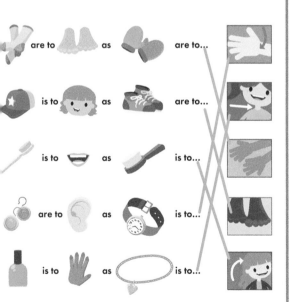

49 Dinnertime

The shark eats:

The cow eats:

The dog eats:

52 Tutti Fruitti

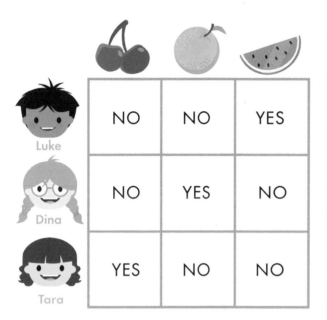

	🍒	🍊	🍉
Luke	NO	NO	YES
Dina	NO	YES	NO
Tara	YES	NO	NO

53 Odd Sound Out

Things that do not belong:

Puzzle 1:

Puzzle 2:

Puzzle 3:

Puzzle 4:

54 I Spy . . .

Row 1:

Row 2:

Row 3:

Row 4:

55 Animal Kingdom

Animals that are not part of the group:

Birds:

Fish:

Insects:

Mammals:

56 Let's Rhyme!

57 Dessert Time!

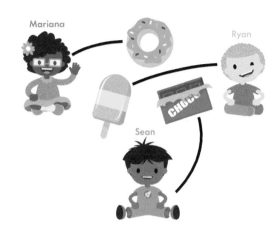

58 A Trip to the Zoo

Amir's favorite animal is the polar bear.

59 Categories

Balls: Add another type of ball.

Fruits: Add another fruit.

Tools: Add another tool.

62 School of Fish

63 Color a Garden

64 Dress Up Time!

Natasha   Leo   Brooke   Matt

65 Birthday Fun

Manny is three years old.

He was two years old last year.

He will be four years old next year.

66 Set the Table

Robin Robin's table has 3 sides.

George George's table has 4 sides. 2 are short and 2 are long.

Nadia Nadia's table has no sides. It is round.

Max Max's table has 4 equal sides.

67 Off to School!

68 Yummy Treats

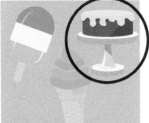

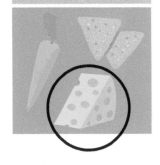

69 Riding Bikes

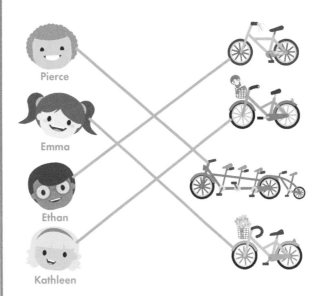

Molly Lynch lives in the San Francisco Bay Area with her husband, JB, and son, Luke. She is an early elementary teacher with nearly two decades of experience. She shares teaching ideas, activities, and resources for busy teachers at Lucky to Be in First (LuckyToBeInFirst.com). She also blogs about her life as a new mom on Lucky & Co (LuckyAndCo.net). In her spare time, Molly loves to read, read, and read even more. She is addicted to shoes, Mexican food, and books.

CPSIA information can be obtained
at www.ICGtesting.com
Printed in the USA
LVHW011908160320
650198LV00001B/1